Another Friday

Peter Lay & Zaiming Wang

Black Eyes Publishing UK

Another Friday
By Peter Lay & Zaiming Wang
© Peter Lay & Zaiming Wang, 2019

Published by Black Eyes Publishing UK, 2019
Brockworth, Gloucestershire, England
www.blackeyespublishinguk.co.uk

ISBN: 978-1-9999583-6-7

Peter Lay & Zaiming Wang have asserted their moral right under the Copyright, Designs and Patents Act, 1988, to be identified as the authors of this work.

All Rights reserved. No part of this publication may be reproduced, copied, stored in a retrieval system, or transmitted, in any form or by any means, without the prior written consent of the copyright holders, nor be otherwise circulated in any form of binding or cover other than that in which it is published and without a similar condition being imposed on the subsequent purchaser.

A CIP catalogue record for this title is available from the British Library.

Cover design: Jason Conway, cre8urbrand.
            www.cre8urbrand.co.uk

Also, by Peter Lay & Zaiming Wang

Yellow Over The Mountain
岭上黄

~

Also, By Peter Lay

Still tilting at Windmills

redbootsman 'Such Strange Philosophies'

'Another Friday' should not be seen as a sequel to 'Yellow Over The Mountain', more of a supplement.

Most of the poems were written collaboratively via exchange of email and text messages.

Coincidently, the title of this book, 'Another Friday' is taken from the poem on page 42... Irony?

Index

Lay Down	9
A Coat	10
Winter	11
Snow White in March in England	12
Expectation	13
Limited	14
Fallen	15
Heat	16
Taste - 味	17
Morning - 黎明	18
Nice - 美	19
Heavy Load	20
Angry or Calm?	21
Mason	22
Nice Bear	23
My Dream	24
Orientation of a Tree	25
Balance?	26
Deep	27
I'm not looking forward to 2019	28
The Stone	29
Just Right	30
The Thin Wall	31
Humble	32
We are not	33
We are lost	34
Days were worn	35
Sad?	36
Scarborough Beach	37
Scarborough Town	38
Different World	39
Like Silk	40
Your Beauty is Poetry	41

Another Friday	42
The Stairs	43
4:24am	44
Today	45
Hello	46
Dark	47
Daylight	48
Crazy?	49

Lay Down
Peter Lay & Zaiming Wang

Come walk with me for a while
Then lay down by my side...

By your side
Lay down
Close eyes
Face to sky
Or sunshine
Hear the snore
By my side

Only one is sleeping...

A Coat
Zaiming Wang & Peter Lay

I'm not looking forward
To Spring

I just expect
Everybody
Have at least
A coat

Living through
Winter

As Winter thaws
Can we escape the coat?
And walk naked
Under the sun...

You are right
Everyone should have
At least a coat
For when they need it....

Winter
Zaiming Wang & Peter Lay

Dark and cold
Winter is biting
Snuggle up inside
Love is warming

No matter the weather,
We can decide
If it is cold or warm

Snow White in March in England
Zaiming Wang & Peter Lay

It is snowing,
Winter enjoys its stay
But Spring comes with warmth
For me both are beautiful

The warmth of Spring
Is late this year
I see the Flower bloom
In her yellow dress,
Needing heat
In winter's bite

Snow gleams occupied March
As the envoy of cold Winter
Testing our faith of warm
If Spring may really not come
How can we get heat?
And look at flower

Expectation
Peter Lay & Zaiming Wang

I awake
Not to the sun
But to clouds
And the expectation
Of rain

I look
For a smile
Brightening the sky
In beautiful eyes
Reflected

The colours of eyes
Are different
The reflection
The same

Limited
Zaiming Wang & Peter Lay

Taking a while
Writing nicely
Showing respect
From inside

Others can be ignored
Time is limited

Open eyes
Heard different voice
Is this world
It is morning

It is morning
Still in bed
Naked…

Fallen
Peter Lay & Zaiming Wang

How the mighty have fallen,
Like a tree crashing down...
Bruised my knee
And pulled my thigh muscle,
By tripping over a stool...
How embarrassing,
I try not to make a habit
Of this sort of thing
Haha ha
It's still quite stiff but improving

You meant it is true
It happened to you?
How the mighty have fallen?
Where and when?

I find out the reason
Why I felt so low
As the gardener absent
Because his knee
And muscle of thigh
And he feels embarrassed...

My knee is much better now
It still aches a bit
But I am walking normally
Well normally for me
If you wanted to catch me
It would be easy for you....

By feet yes, I can easily catch you

Heat
Peter Lay & Zaiming Wang

It's the beginning of a new week
A week of sunshine, heat, heat, heat
Time to stop and take a drink
Slip off your clothes and dance
To the magic of the sultry beat
As kisses generate, yet more heat…

Since the long-time snoring,
The bear at last woke up
In the beginning of the new week…
It is the week I am looking forward to

Taste - 味
Peter Lay & Zaiming Wang

Taste is important
Taste is divine
Taste is artistic
Tasting is mystic

Taste is honey
Taste is heat
Taste is my lips
And yours

品味是何等重要
它是神圣
它是美
和神秘

味道是蜜
是热度
是我的唇
体验
你的

How important is taste
It is sacred
It is beautiful
And mystery

Taste is honey
It is heat
It is my lips
Experience yours

Morning - 黎明
Peter Lay & Zaiming Wang

In the morning
Climb the mountain
Sit upon a tree
And feel it grow

黎明
翻上山顶
坐在枝头

一棵
树
从你心里
长出

Dawn
Turn over the top
Sitting on the branch
A tree
From your heart
Growing out

Nice - 美
Peter Lay & Zaiming Wang

Mould your beauty against me
Look into my eyes
Touch my lips with yours

隔着时空
你看着我
我听着你

Time and space
You look at me
I am listening to you

Heavy Load
Zaiming Wang & Peter Lay

Breathe again
Is not relieved of a heavy load
It is
Your breath
You feel it

I hear you breathing
I see you breathing
Your load is great
Too much to bare

So, the bear will hold you
When he can
He feels your anguish
He feels your pain

Angry or Calm?
Peter Lay & Zaiming Wang

How are things now
Are you angry?
Or feeling calm

Are your senses alive?
Or dulled with pain
As the rain comes

I just feel down.
I didn't talk to him
Since that day
I feel I died
And bury old things

I really think about myself
And I'd like to visit your place
To please myself,
It is the time to love me.

Mason
Zaiming Wang

Naked
Carry sword
Straddle horse.

To be an exhaustive
Knight
I am living in the
After death

The Sword Woman
Seduces my eyes, my mind
Powerful and free...

Nice Bear
Peter Lay & Zaiming Wang

The bear lies naked
In his lonely bed
He is thinking
Of the Yellow Flower

Before the bear thinking of
The yellow flower
Was blooming already

The exquisite beauty
Of the Yellow Flower
Has aroused the desire
And passion of the Bear

Intensely felt...
Same feeling of you
In my mind
How nice bear he is...

My Dream
Zaiming Wang

Have to have a dream and act on it
Once I get my freedom
I am going to fly
I feel my heart is in jail
In heart
Not geographic

It is just dream to please myself
It is very far dream in a far future
But study French is happy thing to do now
Living in the dream I feel happy to enjoy myself

Orientation of a Tree
Zaiming Wang

There is a road sign
On the street
In Paris

Point to east
Point to west

Point to south
Point to north

There is also a tree
On the street
In Paris

It points to the sky

Balance?
Zaiming Wang

The world is keeping the balance...
Bad things on the scale
Human beings are learning fairness, justice and capacity
But the cost is the blood of the innocent.

Indeed...

Deep
Zaiming Wang

Never look at me with your eyes
Neither brain
See me by your heart please
Otherwise
You will see me dimly

Deep sense…

Things going to deep
The only reason why we live
Is looking for who we are
And where…

I'm not looking forward to 2019
Zaiming Wang

I expect
Dates
Blown by wind
Just like
Every single day
Of now

I'm not looking forward
Who
What
When
Where

I expect
Me
Breathe
Now
Here

Feel like a stone thrown into the lake, the waves disturbing the quiet and peace, it recovers now but this water is not that water any more...

The Stone
Zaiming Wang

In time everything changes...
New lake
New water
Could rejuvenate the stone

Just Right
Zaiming Wang

My raised right hand
Staying in the air
For longer
Neither more nor less
Just right
In this morning
While crossing
The cross street

The Thin Wall
Zaiming Wang

The thin wall
Making a house
For flowers
The Person
Standing
Outside

Humble
Zaiming Wang

Humble
Is the thoroughfare
Through
To the peak
Of the mountain

Humble but true

We are not
Zaiming Wang

We are not as we thought
Walking in the streets
We think we are everything.

The world is big
Just big as how
You have seen

We are lost
Peter Lay

We are lost
In the oceans
Of time

Nearly drowning
As we fight
Against the tide

Days were worn
Zaiming Wang

Days were worn

Doing something
Breadwinning

Clock hanging
On the wall

Walking anticlockwise
Stolen everything

Sad?
Zaiming Wang

You have asked me are you feeling sad.
I changed my face pretending to smile.
You said it's all right if you feel sad.

This makes me have a poem

Don't mend dreariness
Never even thinking of

Poignant just behind
It is not happening
In the past and present

What I want to say is
'It is not always happening
In the past and future'

Scarborough Beach
Zaiming Wang

I picked up the gravels
The word and sentence
Drilling in between

I drank coffee
They went into body

I walked
They roll under shoes

I talked
They be quiet

I breathe
They blocked in nose

I closed eyes
They flew

I took pen
They gone

Scarborough Town
Peter Lay

In Scarborough Town
The Bear and the Flower
Cast shadows on the beach
As we stooped to pick stones from the sand
Washed clean by the receding tide

As we walked along the strand
We dived into alleyways and onto quays
Looking for pictures
For our phones
You posed
Arched your body
I clicked

We drove up steep hills
My hand on the gear stick
To the castle and Anne Bronte's grave
And on the cliff path
We circled around circular houses
People like ants below

Different World
Zaiming Wang

When she looks at me

Everybody living in a different world

Human beings, faces like blades

Cutting?

Like Silk
Zaiming Wang

Lips, hands, fingers

Touch

Skin

Like silk

Slides smooth

Entwines

Tie a knot

Tight

To combine in one

Moment

Forever

Your Beauty is Poetry
Peter Lay & Zaiming Wang

Your beauty is poetry
Spoken in a look

Squeeze squeeze

Harder harder

Hihi hihi

Kiss kiss

Another Friday
Zaiming Wang & Peter Lay

Another Friday, no tears
No sunshine as well.
What a good Friday
And weekends sometime in life...

No sunshine
The sky is crying
Life is dying
Slowly over years

Beauty holds me
Rejuvenates me
Loves me
Through her tears

'Last Friday' is always a good one
This Friday sad
Life is up and down
Up and down is life

Before dying
We all will see
How much beautiful
The life will be
How much expecting
The minds did

We learn to enjoy
Every precious moment
Every thought
Every touch
Every feeling
Every pleasure
Then as we are dying - We are living

The Stairs
Zaiming Wang

The stairs
There are three
Plus, my feet
Become four
Upwards
Closer to the sky

4:24am
Peter Lay & Zaiming Wang

Just woke up,
It's 4:24am...
I am remembering
Our trip to Scarborough,
Strolling along the sand, collecting stones
The sun bright
Making shadows
To photograph
We were happy
Laughing and talking
Exploring alleyways
You posed on the steps
The shutter clicked...

St. Mary's church and Scarborough castle
They are on the top of the hill
Named Paradise
Above the sea level for a mile

Where Ann Bronte lies at rest
Her headstone battered by winds - replaced

Today
Zaiming Wang

Today is a point
Which is converged
By whole life
I'd like give
A 'quotation mark'
to him
'Today'

Hello
Peter Lay & Zaiming Wang

Hello Ming

Brrr its cold
Can you feel the bite?
Of the jaws of winter
In the night...

Hello Peter
Hello winter

Cold is my season
Cause I am from
Summer

I was made
To be a breath
Up and flying

Fold your wings
And snuggle down
It will be a while
Until spring comes around...

Dark
Peter Lay & Zaiming Wang

Laying in my bed
It's still dark
But morning has come
And I am awake
Alone and naked
With my thoughts

It is dark
'Cause the ring covers the light

Others can be ignored
Thoughts make life alive

Daylight
Peter Lay

Daylight stretches
Equinox approaches
The amorous Bear
Aroused from slumber
Seeks out the Flower
With love and hunger

Crazy?
Peter Lay

Are you crazy?
Yes of course.
You are a beautiful
Kind of crazy.
Full of amazing ideas,
And wonderful dreams.
So, if you are crazy,
Then I am crazy too.

Sleep beckons
On angel wings
Tired eyes
And sweetest dreams

Goodnight
Sweet Flower,
Beautiful
Inspiring
Crazy
Together
In dreams...

'Yellow Over The Mountain' is a unique book, the dual text is in English and Chinese. It is a delicate and touching dialogue between two people of two cultures; an amalgam of East and West. Taken from the actual texts and emails over a 4-month period, this metaphorical journey seeks to temper sadness through the joy of creation.

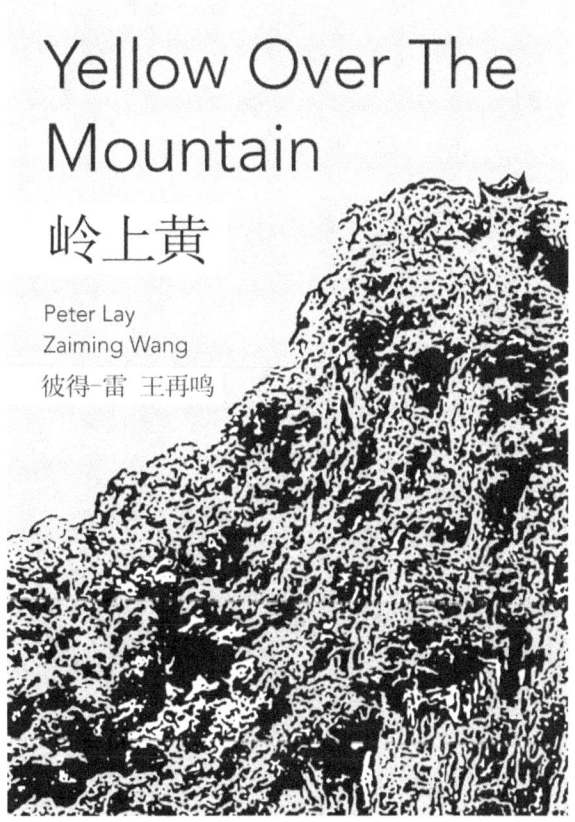

ISBN: 978-1-9999583-0-5

These two people attempt to ameliorate daily reality and it's struggles through a combined philosophy of art and performance. The world they create is a magical place, where the beauty of both cultures combines to create a unique mythical story that will stand the test of time.

Life is a performance.
Silas Marne, April 2018

www.ingramcontent.com/pod-product-compliance
Lightning Source LLC
Chambersburg PA
CBHW052126070526
44586CB00016B/2107